How to Make

HAWAIIAN
RIBBON Leis

A Step-by-Step Guide

How to Make
HAWAIIAN RIBBON Leis

A Step-by-Step Guide

Coreen Mikioi Iwamoto

Jim Widess

MUTUAL PUBLISHING

Library of Congress Catalog Card
Number: 2002108990

First Printing, October 2002
Second Printing, July 2003
Third Printing, January 2004
3 4 5 6 7 8 9

ISBN 1-56647-575-9

Photography by Jim Widess
Cover design by Danvers Fletcher
Layout design by Sistenda Yim

MUTUAL PUBLISHING
1215 Center Street, Suite 210
Honolulu, Hawai'i 96816
Ph: (808) 732-1709 Fax: (808) 734-4094
e-mail: mutual@lava.net
www.mutualpublishing.com

Printed in Korea

Table of Contents

Acknowledgments

Mahalo to Margie, her contemporary mentors and crafting peers, for their Hawaiian-ness in sharing this evolving craft. Mahalo also to both my Honolulu and Bay Area families for supporting my process of learning about, living and teaching Hawaiiana. And ultimately, to my mother Betty, who nurtured any craftsmanship I have by her example, my aloha to you. I hope to be as good as you when I grow up.

—Mikioi

To Sher, (Leialoha), my wife and Hawaiian inspiration and our son Andy, thank you for your support for this project.

To that fantastic staff of The Caning Shop—Shelly, Jenny, Lerryn, Andre, and Tammi—thank you for allowing us the time to photograph these leis.

To our Aunties and friends on Kaua'i, thank you for all your lessons.

—Jim

Introduction

Growing up as a kamaʻāina (child of the land) of Hawaiʻi, one can easily believe that the vibrant tropical flowers prevalent in the Islands are readily available throughout the world. Moving to California changed that naïve view. Because of physical separation from the land of my birth, I have gained a greater appreciation for the lush fragrances, hues and textures of Hawaiʻi's flowers and plants.

As I continued my education of "things Hawaiian" in the San Francisco Bay Area, I was introduced to old and new Hawaiian crafts. One of these was ribbon lei-making. In past generations, tūtūwahine (grandmothers) would pass down this handcraft to their moʻopuna (grandchildren), using rudimentary materials such as rick-rack. My mother taught me how to make these types of ribbon leis.

With the advent of synthetic materials, different types of ribbons became available to fashion new styles of ribbon leis. Crafty individuals, especially in Hawaiʻi, used these ribbons to create leis that looked more like their real-life models. Two of these crafters are Carole Mito and Coryn Tanaka, both of Honolulu, who continue to be strong proponents of this craft. They teach ribbon lei-making classes on Oʻahu; one of their students is my sister-in-law, Marjorie Jo Iwamoto, who in turn has taught me additional styles and techniques via long-distance. She and I toss around ideas for new lei styles, as well, and share our discoveries and patterns.

This is just one example of how Hawaiian crafts have survived for centuries. And more contemporary crafts, like Hawaiian ribbon lei-making, can continue to be passed on, from person to person, from generation to generation, through this type of sharing. So in this spirit, we share with you some of the techniques of Hawaiian ribbon lei-making, and encourage you to share your discoveries with the next person.

Coreen "Mikioi" Iwamoto

Ruler Templates For Ribbon

3/8"

1"

1-1/2"

2"

2-1/2"

How to Make Hawaiian Ribbon Leis—
A Step-by-Step Guide
by Coreen Mikioi Iwamoto
and Jim Widess

ʻIlima

ʻIlima detail

ʻIlima (Sida flower)

—Materials Needed—

This lei design was created by Carole Mito of Honolulu.

- 25 to 30 yds. 5/8" Offray yellow gold satin ribbon
- 10 ft. beading or upholstery thread
- 1 sewing needle
- Aoyama 1/8" double-sided tape (optional)
- Scissors
- Ruler
- Marking pen (preferably gel-style to prevent spreading ink)
- 1 wooden clothespin with metal spring

1) Satin ribbon has a shiny side and a dull side.

3) Thread your sewing needle with the beading or upholstery thread, and bring cut ends together. Tie a double knot approximately 3 to 4" from the cut ends. This amount of thread will allow you to complete a finished lei of 40", with additional thread to easily tie the ends together. Clamp the clothespin on the very end of your thread beyond the knot, for added weight.

Lay the ribbon in your hand, right side up and cut edge closest to you. Poke needle up through the first pen mark on the ribbon.

2) Lay the satin ribbon on top of or beside a ruler, shiny side up. Allowing for a very short amount of leader at the beginning of the ribbon, dot your ribbon at 3/8" intervals down the ribbon, approximately 1/8" from the edge. If you sew with your right hand, mark the right edge of the ribbon (with the cut edge facing you); if you sew with your left hand, mark the left edge. These are your stitching marks.

(Optional: If you want to make the cut edge of the ribbon resistant to fraying, attach a small piece of Aoyama 1/8" double-sided tape to the wrong side of the cut edge, and fold over the edge to encase the tape, resulting in a clean edge that won't ravel.)

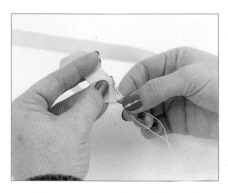

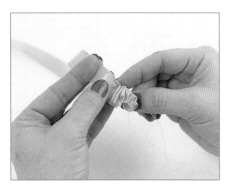

4) Your next stitch will be down through the next pen mark.

5) Continue with this running stitch pattern for several more stitches.

6) Pull the sewn ribbon down the thread until you reach the knotted end.

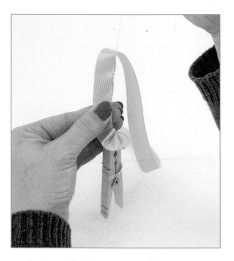

7) Then pull down in small segments at a time, to create gentle little folds as you gather the ribbon, until you have pulled down all of the sewn ribbon. The clothespin will spin a little as your ribbon forms a spiral pattern.

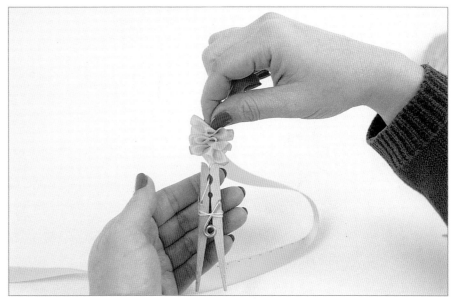

8) This spiral pattern will have 5 to 6 gentle folds in each layer. Be sure to pull the ribbon down toward the knotted end of the thread, to ensure a consistent pattern and to hide the folds and thread.

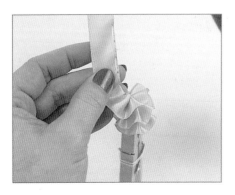

9) Continue this process, with more running stitches, then gathering at the bottom into little folds, until your lei measures 40".

10) Tightly knot the needle end of the thread close against the ribbon.

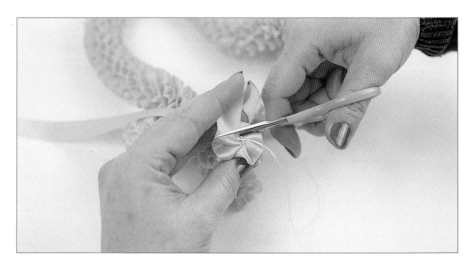

11) Cut needle off of the thread, approximately 3 to 4" away from the knot.

12) Cut off the excess ribbon on the diagonal near the knot.

(Optional: If you want to make the last edge of the ribbon resistant to fraying, attach a small piece of Aoyama 1/8" double-sided tape to the wrong side of the cut edge, and fold over the edge to encase the tape, resulting in a clean edge that won't ravel.)

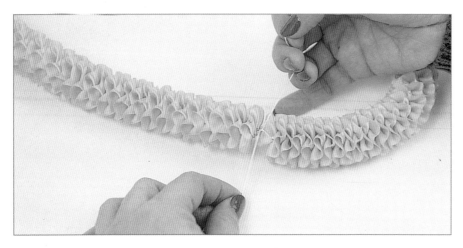

13) Tie both ends of the thread together to form your lei. Make several knots in the same place to prevent the thread from loosening. Trim the thread close to the knots.

14) Tie a decorative ribbon bow on to your lei over your thread knots, to cover up this area and to complete your lei.

1) Cut a 12″ length of 1/2″-wide acetate ribbon, on the diagonal. This will be the binding ribbon.

2) For the bow portion, about 3 to 4″ from the end of the ribbon (shiny side up), make a tight half-twist in the ribbon. This will now expose the dull side of the ribbon after the twist. Hold this twist between your thumb and forefinger. All subsequent twists will be held in this fashion.

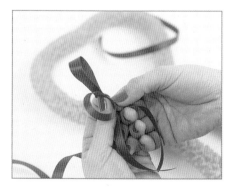

3) Make a top loop, which will become the center of the bow.

4) Once this loop is also secured between your thumb and forefinger, make another half-twist, thus exposing the shiny side again.

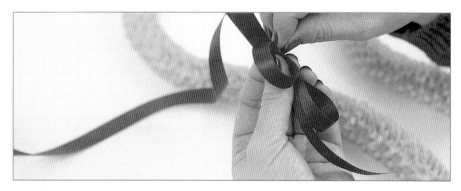

5) Now create a loop on the far side of the center loop, again securing the end between thumb and forefinger and twisting to expose the shiny side.

6) Now create a same-sized loop on the near side of the center loop, again securing the end between thumb and forefinger and twisting to expose the shiny side.

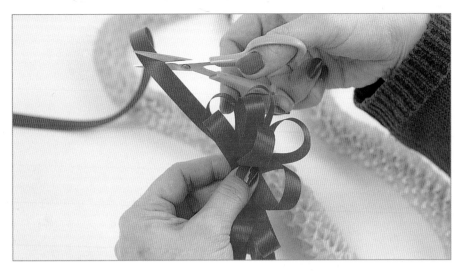

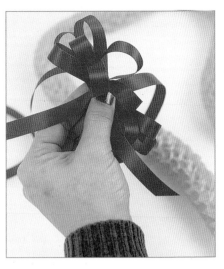

7) Continue creating loops on the far and near sides of the center loop, until you have 5 to 6 on each side. Cut off ribbon about 3 to 4" away from the central twisted area.

8) Feed the binding ribbon through the central loop, shiny side up, and tie into a knot underneath the whole central twisted area.

9) Use the binding ribbon to secure the bow to your lei.

Pīkake

Pīkake detail

Pīkake (Jasmine)

—Materials Needed—

This lei design was created by Carole Mito of Honolulu.

- 40 yds. 3/16″ cream, ivory, antique white or candle-light picot ribbon
- 10 ft. beading or uphol-stery thread
- 1 sewing needle
- Scissors
- 1 wooden clothespin with metal spring

Thread your sewing needle with the beading or uphol-stery thread, and bring cut ends together. Tie a double knot approximately 3 to 4″ from the cut ends. This amount of thread will allow you to complete a finished lei of 40″, with additional thread to easily tie the ends together.

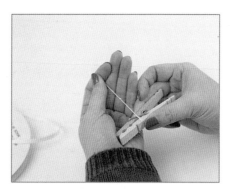

1) Starting from the knotted end of the thread, wind the thread around the center of the clothespin until your thread measures about 4 to 5″ from the needle.

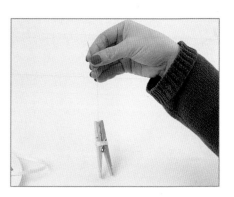

2) Secure the thread in the pincher of the clothespin. You will be working with only 4 to 5″ of thread at a time, letting out additional thread as necessary and pushing the finished petals of the lei downward toward the clothespin as you go.

3) Lay the ribbon in your hand, cut edge closest to you and right side up. You will regulate your stitch length by counting the loops along one edge of the ribbon. Each stitch will be six loops after the last stitch, which should equate to 1″ intervals. Be sure to count only on one edge of the ribbon, since these loops typically alternate and do not line up equally on both edges of the ribbon. Stitching in the center of the ribbon, poke the needle up at a point aligning with a loop. Pull needle toward you while you pull the ribbon away from you (the clothespin should be kept free and dangling—this will keep a weight on your thread, and prevent tangling of the thread with your ribbon and lei design).

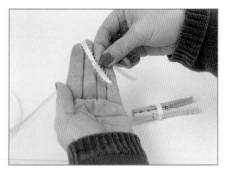

4) Bring your needle up and over the ribbon, and then your next stitch will be up through the center of the ribbon, six loops past your first stitch.

5) Be sure to pull the needle toward you, ribbon away from you, with the clothes-pin dangling.

6) As you pull, the ribbon will form the first of five petals in a loop.

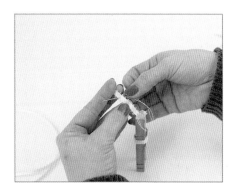

7) Continue with the next stitch, again pulling needle and ribbon in opposite directions to form the next loop.

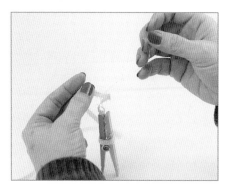

8) The next three stitches continue in this pattern, resulting in a five-point star shape.

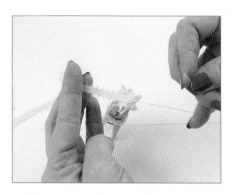

9) The next petal (#6) will start the next row. This petal will be situated between two petals in the previous row. This next row of five petals will alternate with the first row's petals, and your lei will continue on in this star-shaped, alternating pattern.

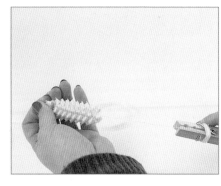

10) As you continue creating rows of petals, you will find that your thread is now too short to continue stitching. Let out a few more inches of thread from the clothespin and clamp it. Gently pull the petals, a little bit at a time, down the thread toward the clothespin.

11) You now have more available thread with which to continue sewing. Continue this process until your lei measures 40".

12) Tightly knot the needle end of the thread close against the ribbon. Cut needle off of the thread, approximately 3 to 4" away from the knot.

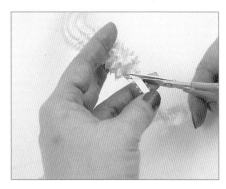

13) Cut away excess ribbon on a diagonal, to prevent raveling.

14) Tie both ends of the thread together to form your lei. Make several knots in the same place to prevent the thread from loosening. Trim the thread close to the knots. Tie a decorative ribbon bow on to your lei over your thread knots to cover up this area and to complete your lei.

Aloalo Hua Moa lei

Aloalo Hua Moa detail

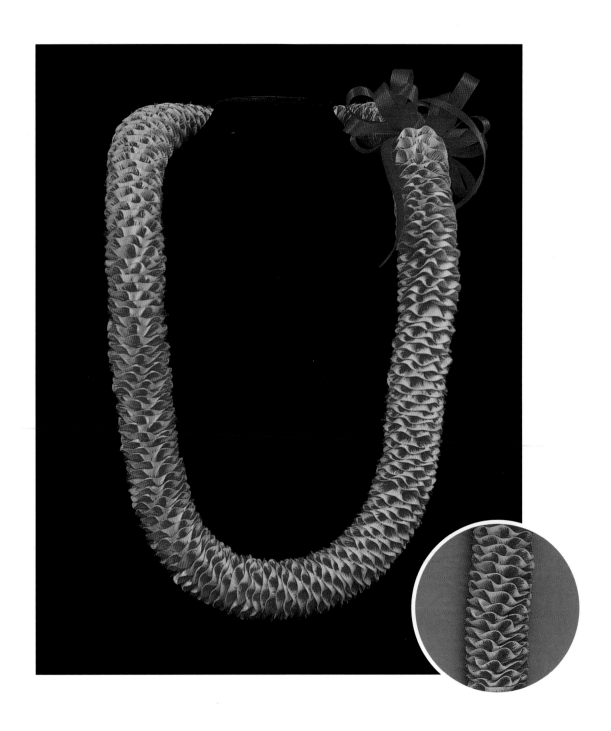

Aloalo Hua Moa or
Aloalo Pele (Lantern 'Ilima)

—Materials Needed—

This lei design was created by Carole Mito of Honolulu.

- 30 yds. #5 (7/8″) red acetate ribbon
- 30 yds. 7/8″ light gold grosgrain ribbon
- 10 ft. beading or upholstery thread
- 1 sewing needle
- 1 sturdy needle (like a carpet needle)
- Aoyama 1/8″ double-sided tape (optional)
- Scissors
- Ruler

1) Cut acetate ribbon into 2′ lengths.

2) Hold a ribbon segment in your hand, right side up, while the other holds the sturdy needle. You are going to shred one side of the ribbon. Poke the needle near the upper right corner of the ribbon. Pull needle away from your other hand, allowing the long strands of the ribbon to pull away with it.

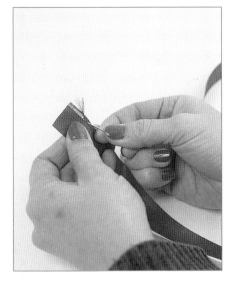

3) Repeat a little further down the long edge of the ribbon, pulling away to reveal more of the loose strands.

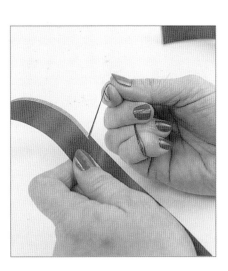

4) When you have pulled away enough of the loose strands to grasp them in your hand, pull them away from the rest of the ribbon.

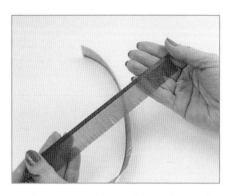

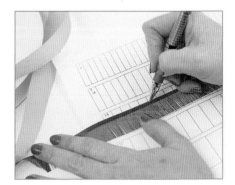

5) Continue with the shredding, pulling away about 1/8″ of strands at a time (pulling more may rip the strands as they pull away from the ribbon).

6) Continue until you leave about 1/4″ of intact ribbon on one side.

7) Lay the intact base of the red ribbon on top of or beside a ruler, right side up. Allowing for a very short amount of leader at the beginning of the ribbon, dot your ribbon at 3/8″ intervals down the ribbon, approximately 1/8″ from the edge of the ribbon. These are your stitching marks.

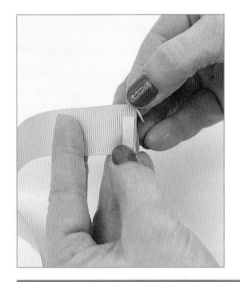

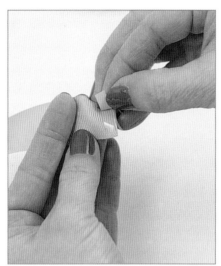

8) (Optional: If you want to make the cut edge of the grosgrain ribbon resistant to fraying, attach a small piece of Aoyama 1/8″ double-sided tape to the wrong side of the cut edge, and fold over the edge to encase the tape, resulting in a clean edge that won't ravel.)

Thread your sewing needle with the beading or upholstery thread, and bring cut ends together. Tie a double knot approximately 3 to 4″ from the cut ends. This amount of thread will allow you to complete a finished lei of 40″, with additional thread to easily tie the ends together.

9) Lay the grosgrain ribbon in your hand, right side up. Lay the shredded ribbon on top of the picot ribbon, right side up, with the intact edge of the shredded ribbon extending slightly outside the edge of the grosgrain ribbon.

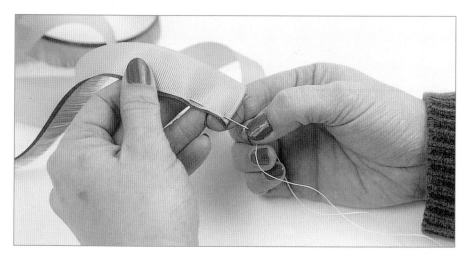

10) Stitching through both ribbons, poke needle up through the first pen mark on the red ribbon. Your next stitch will be down through the next pen mark through both thicknesses. Continue with this running stitch pattern for several more stitches. Be sure to catch both ribbons on every stitch. Seen from the back of the ribbons (above), the red edge sticks out a little from the grosgrain.

11) Firmly gather the sewn ribbon down the thread until you reach the knotted end.

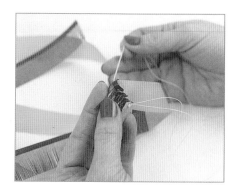

12) Holding both ends of the gathered ribbon near the flush "base", twist the gathers, with one hand turning toward you and the other hand turning outward, to start a spiral pattern to the ribbon.

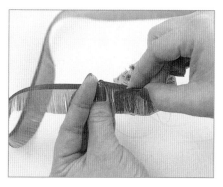

13) This will be a significantly tight spiral, forcing the flower to form more of a cup shape with slight overlaps toward the knotted end of the lei.

14) The red "veins" will end just below the ruffled edge of the finished flower. Be sure to push down the ribbon toward the knotted end as you twist, to ensure a consistently tight pattern.

15) Continue this process, with several more running stitches, gathering, and twisting, until you come to the end of the shredded ribbon.

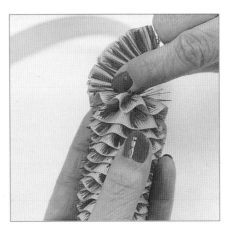

16) Overlap the end of that shredded ribbon with another new ribbon, and for the next few stitches you will be sewing through three thicknesses (the grosgrain ribbon, the old shredded ribbon, and the new shredded ribbon) to secure the new ribbon to your lei.

17) Continue this process, with more running stitches, gathering, twisting into a cup shape, pushing down toward the knotted end, and adding more shredded ribbon, until your lei measures 40″.

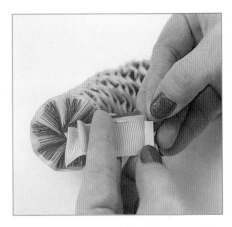

18) Cut off the excess acetate ribbon past your last stitch. Cut off the excess grosgrain ribbon past your last stitch, about 1/4″ beyond the cut acetate ribbon.

19) (Optional: If you want to make the last edge of the grosgrain ribbon resistant to fraying, attach a small piece of Aoyama 1/8″ double-sided tape to the wrong side of the cut edge, and fold over the edge to encase the tape, resulting in a clean edge that won't ravel.)

20) Tightly knot the needle end of the thread close against the ribbon. Cut needle off of the thread, approximately 3 to 4″ away from the knot.

21) Tie both ends of the thread together to form your lei. Make several knots in the same place to prevent the thread from loosening. Trim the thread close to the knots. Tie a decorative ribbon bow on to your lei over your thread knots, to cover up this area and to complete your lei.

ʻĀkulikuli (ʻĀkulikuli detail)

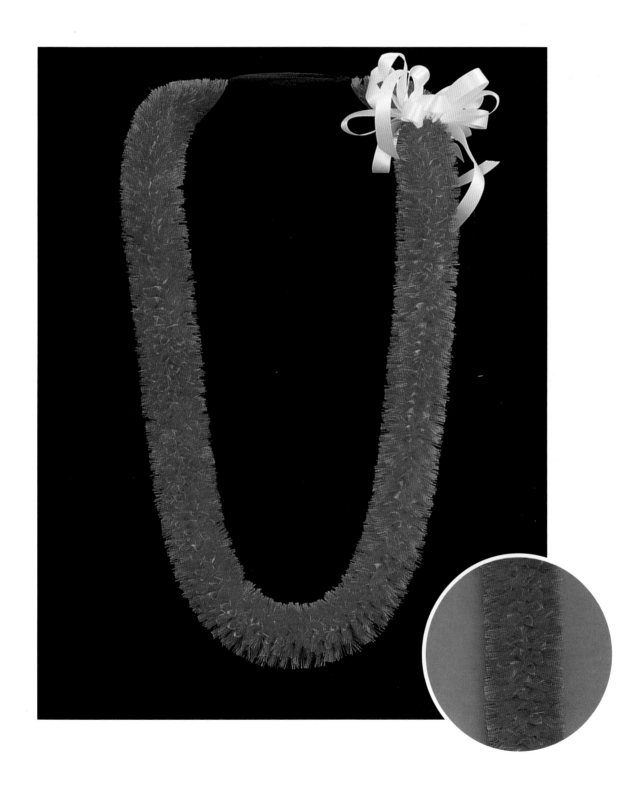

'Ākulikuli (Ice Plant)

—Materials Needed—

This lei design was created by Carole Mito of Honolulu.

- 25 yds. #5 (7/8″) cyclamen or fuchsia acetate ribbon
- 25 yd. 5/8″ fuchsia picot ribbon
- 10 ft. beading or upholstery thread
- 1 sewing needle
- 1 sturdy needle (like a carpet needle)
- Aoyama 1/8″ double-sided tape (optional)
- Scissors

1) Cut acetate ribbon into 24″ lengths.

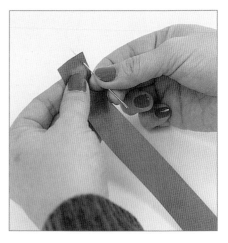

2) Hold a ribbon segment in your hand, right side up, while the other holds the sturdy needle. You are going to shred one side of the ribbon. Poke the needle near the upper right corner of the ribbon 1/8″ from the edge.

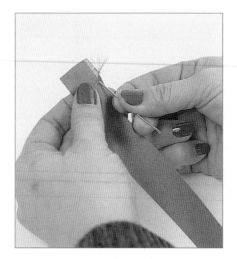

3) Pull needle away from your other hand, allowing the long strands of the ribbon to pull away with it. Repeat a little further down the long edge of the ribbon, pulling away to reveal more of the loose strands.

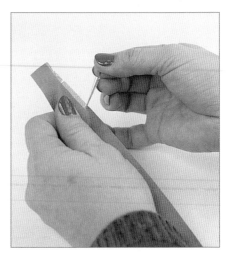

4) When you have pulled away enough of the loose strands to grasp them in your hand, pull them away from the rest of the ribbon.

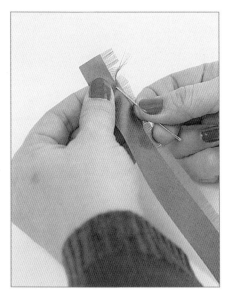

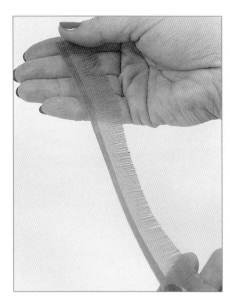

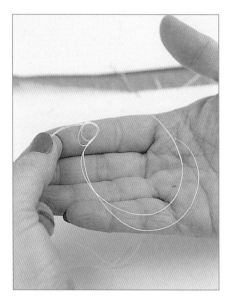

5) Continue with the shredding, pulling away about 1/8″ of strands at a time (pulling more may rip the strands as they pull away from the ribbon).

Continue until you leave about 1/4″ of intact ribbon on one side.

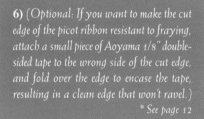

6) (Optional: If you want to make the cut edge of the picot ribbon resistant to fraying, attach a small piece of Aoyama 1/8″ double-sided tape to the wrong side of the cut edge, and fold over the edge to encase the tape, resulting in a clean edge that won't ravel.)
* See page 12

7) Thread your sewing needle with the beading or upholstery thread, and bring cut ends together. Tie a double knot approximately 3 to 4″ from the cut ends. This amount of thread will allow you to complete a finished lei of 40″, with additional thread to easily tie the ends together.

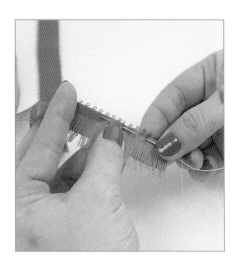

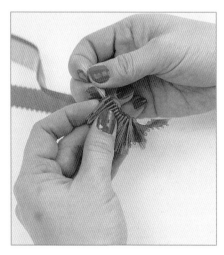

8) Lay the fuchsia picot ribbon in your hand, wrong side up. Lay the shredded ribbon on top of the picot ribbon, right side up, with the intact edge of the shredded ribbon flush with the edge of the picot ribbon. The loops of the picot ribbon will be visible from beyond the acetate ribbon.

9) You will regulate your stitch length by counting the loops on the flush edge of the picot ribbon. Each stitch will be two loops after the last stitch, which should equate to 3/8″ intervals. Be sure to count only on that one flush side of the ribbon, since these loops typically alternate and do not line up equally on both edges of the ribbon.

10) Stitching close to the flush edge of both ribbons, poke needle up through both thicknesses. Your next stitch will be two loops away from that stitch. Continue with this running stitch pattern for several more stitches. Be sure to catch both ribbons on every stitch.

11) Firmly gather the sewn ribbon down the thread until you reach the knotted end.

12) Holding both ends of the gathered ribbon near the flush "base", twist the gathers, with one hand turning toward you and the other hand turning outward, to start a spiral pattern to the ribbon.

13) This spiral pattern will have 5 to 6 gentle folds in each layer. Be sure to push down the ribbon toward the knotted end as you twist, to ensure a consistently tight pattern.

14) Continue this process, with several more running stitches, gathering, and twisting, until you come to the end of the shredded ribbon.

15) Overlap the end of that shredded ribbon with another new ribbon, and for the next few stitches you will be sewing through three thicknesses (the picot ribbon, the old shredded ribbon, and the new shredded ribbon) to secure the new ribbon to your lei.

16) Continue this process, with more running stitches, gathering, twisting, and adding more shredded ribbon, until your lei measures 40". Cut off the excess acetate ribbon after your last stitch. Cut off the excess picot ribbon after your last stitch, leaving about 1/4" excess.

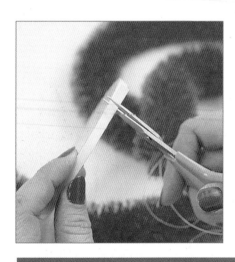

17) *(Optional: If you want to make the last edge of the picot ribbon resistant to fraying, attach a small piece of Aoyama 1/8" double-sided tape to the wrong side of the cut edge, and fold over the edge to encase the tape, resulting in a clean edge that won't ravel.)*

18) Tightly knot the needle end of the thread close against the ribbon. Cut needle off of the thread, approximately 3 to 4″ away from the knot.

19) Tie both ends of the thread together to form your lei.

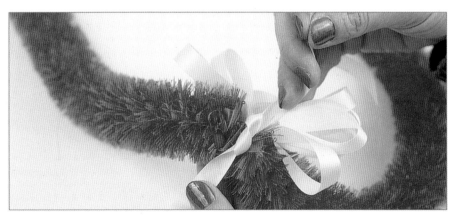

20) Make several knots in the same place to prevent the thread from loosening.

21) Trim the thread close to the knots.

22) Tie a decorative ribbon bow on to your lei over your thread knots, to cover up this area and to complete your lei.

'Ohai Ali'i Piki ('Ohai Ali'i Piki detail)

'Ohai Ali'i Piki (Peach Poinciana)

—Materials Needed—

This lei design was created by Coryn Tanaka of Honolulu.

- 10 yds. #3 (5/8″) picardy acetate ribbon
- 10 yds. #3 (5/8″) orchid acetate ribbon
- 7 yds. #3 (5/8″) yellow acetate ribbon
- 10 yds. #3 (5/8″) peach acetate ribbon
- 1-1/2 yds. #100 (4″) pink acetate ribbon
- 10 ft. beading or upholstery thread
- 1 sewing needle
- 1 sturdy needle (like a carpet needle)
- Scissors
- Ruler

1) Lay the picardy acetate ribbon on top or beside a ruler. At 1-1/2″ intervals, fan-fold the ribbon back and forth, to mark your cutting lengths.

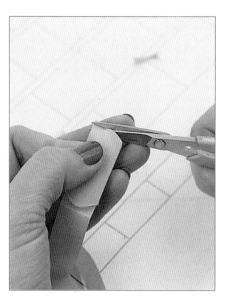

2) When you have a comfortable amount of ribbon folded, cut the folded edge in a half-circle shape. Repeat with the other side. Each cut piece is a petal of the flower. Continue cutting this 1-1/2″ shape of the picardy, orchid and peach ribbons, to make at least 240 picardy, 240 orchid and 240 peach petals.

3) Measuring 1″, cut the same shape of the yellow ribbon to make at least 240 yellow petals.

4) You will now prepare the stamens. Measuring 2″, fan-fold the #100 pink ribbon to create six "panels." Cut the ribbon, which should measure 12″ total.

5) Open up the folded pink ribbon, fold down its center line, "wrong" sides together, and crease down this 12" length.

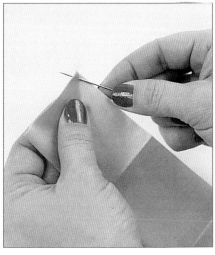

6) Hold the creased edge in your hand, while the other holds the sturdy needle. You are going to shred the edge of the ribbon. Poke the needle near the upper right corner of the ribbon, through both thicknesses.

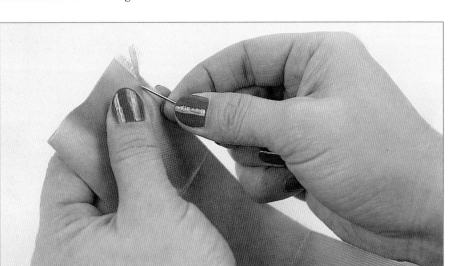

7) Pull needle away from your other hand, allowing the long strands of the ribbon to pull away with it. Repeat a little further down the long edge of the ribbon, pulling away to reveal more of the loose strands.

8) When you have pulled away enough of the loose strands to grasp them in your hand, pull them away from the rest of the ribbon.

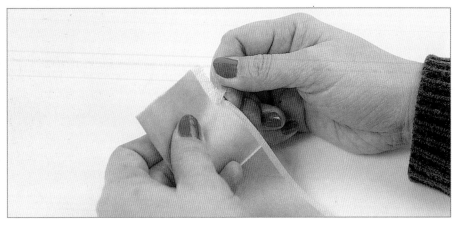

9) Continue with the shredding, pulling away about 1/8" of strands at a time (pulling more may rip the strands as they pull away from the ribbon).

10) Continue until you leave about 1/4" of intact ribbon, on each side of the long crease.

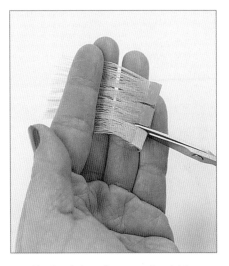

11) At each 2″ interval you originally fan-folded, cut the 1/4″ "spine." You should have six 2″ pieces. (The markings on the ribbon should not be made on your lei; they are merely indications of the measurements you will be cutting.)

12) For each of these 2″ pieces, cut in half to yield twelve 1″ pieces.

13) Each of the 1″ pieces should be cut into thirds. You should now have six pieces of 1/3″ shred from that initial 2″ panel of ribbon. These represent the stamens of the flower. Repeat with additional 12″ sections of pink ribbon as needed.

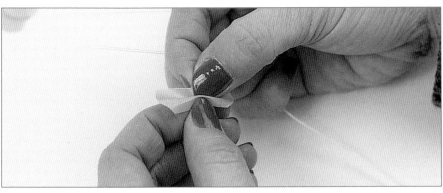

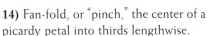

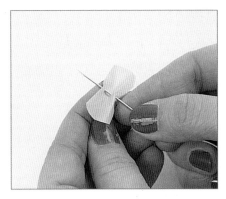

Thread your sewing needle with the beading or upholstery thread, and bring cut ends together. Tie a double knot approximately 3 to 4″ from the cut ends. This amount of thread will allow you to complete a finished lei of 40″, with additional thread to easily tie the ends together.

14) Fan-fold, or "pinch," the center of a picardy petal into thirds lengthwise.

15) Poke your needle through the center of the petal, through all three thicknesses. Continue with one more picardy petal. All of the petals will be sewn in this "pinch" fashion.

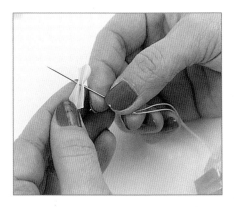

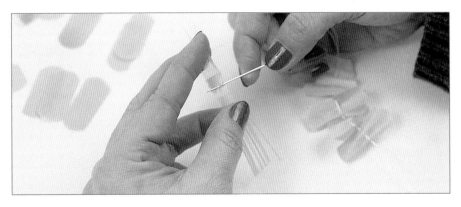

16) Pinch and sew the centers of two orchid petals, then two yellow petals.

17) Take one of the shredded pink ribbon pieces, and open it up to reveal the spine and crease. Using a tiny running stitch, sew up the crease of the spine.

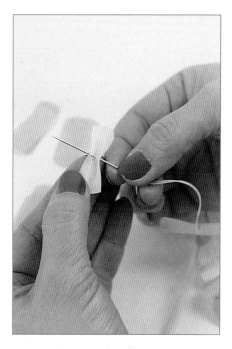

18) Pinch and sew the centers of two peach petals.

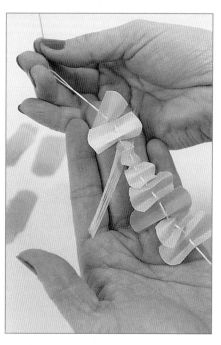

19) Gather the petals and pink shred together. This will make one flower in your lei.

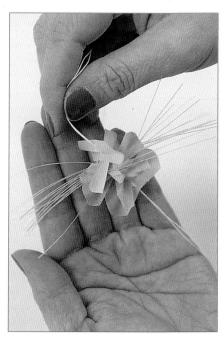

20) Pull these petals down toward your knot at the end of the thread. Be sure to alternate the petals so they cross over each other to hide the folds and thread.

21) Continue with this series, using two picardy, two orchid, two yellow, one pink shred, and two peach, until your lei measures 40″.

22) Tightly knot the needle end of the thread close against the ribbon. Cut needle off of the thread, approximately 3-4″ away from the knot.

23) Tie both ends of the thread together to form your lei. Make several knots in the same place to prevent the thread from loosening. Trim the thread close to the knots. Tie a decorative ribbon bow onto your lei over your thread knots, to cover up this area and to complete your lei.

ʻAwapuhi Keʻokeʻo

ʻAwapuhi Keʻokeʻo

'Awapuhi Ke'oke'o (White Ginger)

—Materials Needed—

This lei design was created by Margie Iwamoto of Honolulu.

- 36 yds. #3 (5/8″) ivory acetate ribbon
- 18 yds. #3 (5/8″) eggshell acetate ribbon
- 5 yds. #3 (5/8″) yellow acetate ribbon
- 1 yds. #40 (2-1/2″) white acetate ribbon
- 10 ft. beading or upholstery thread
- 1 sewing needle
- 1 sturdy needle (like a carpet needle)
- Scissors
- Ruler

1) Lay the ivory acetate ribbon on top or beside a ruler. At 2-1/2″ intervals, fan-fold the ribbon back and forth, to mark your cutting lengths.

2) When you have a comfortable amount of ribbon folded, cut the folded edge in a half-circle shape. Repeat with the other side. Continue cutting this 2-1/2″ shape of the ivory and eggshell ribbons, to make at least 1,300 ivory and 650 eggshell pieces, or petals.

3) Measuring 1″, cut the same shape of the yellow ribbon, to make at least 160 petals of this color.

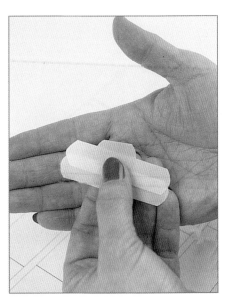

4) These are the three main petals for your flowers. You will now prepare the stamens.

5) Measuring 2″, fan fold the white ribbon to create six "panels."

6) Cut the ribbon, which should measure 12″ total.

7) Open up the folded white ribbon, fold down its center line, wrong sides together, and crease down this 12″ length.

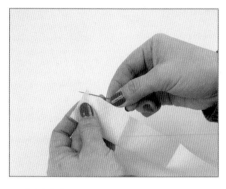

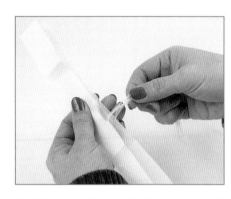

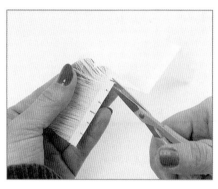

8) Hold the creased edge in your hand, while the other holds the sturdy needle. You are going to shred the edge of the ribbon. Poke the needle near the upper right corner of the ribbon, through both thicknesses. Pull needle away from your other hand, allowing the long strands of the ribbon to pull away with it. Repeat a little further down the long edge of the ribbon, pulling away to reveal more of the loose strands.

9) When you have pulled away enough of the loose strands to grasp them in your hand, pull them away from the rest of the ribbon. Continue with the shredding, pulling away about 1/8″ of strands at a time (pulling more may rip the strands as they pull away from the ribbon). Continue until you leave about 1/4″ of intact ribbon, on each side of the long crease.

10) At each 2″ interval you originally fan folded, cut the 1/4″ "spine." You should have six 2″ pieces. (The markings on the ribbon should not be made on your lei; they are merely indications of the measurements you will be cutting.)

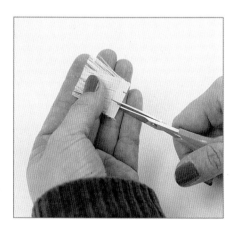

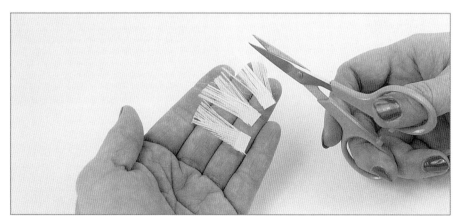

11) For each of these 2″ pieces, cut in half to yield twelve 1″ pieces.

12) Each of the 1″ pieces should be cut into thirds. You should now have 6 pieces of 1/3″ shred from that initial 2″ panel of ribbon. These represent the stamens of the flower. Repeat with additional 12″ sections of white ribbon as needed.

Thread your sewing needle with the beading or upholstery thread, and bring cut ends together. Tie a double knot approximately 3 to 4" from the cut ends. This amount of thread will allow you to complete a finished lei of 40", with additional thread to easily tie the ends together.

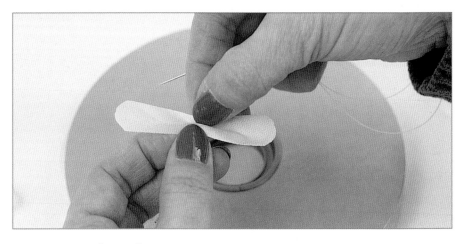

13) Fan-fold, or "pinch," the center of an ivory petal into thirds lengthwise.

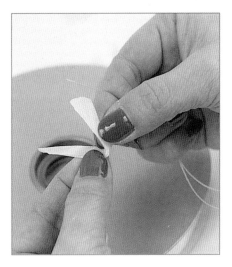

14) Fold this in half crosswise into a tight "V" shape.

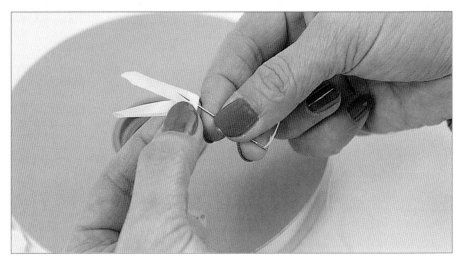

15) Poke your needle through all six thicknesses. Repeat with seven more ivory petals, alternating the petals so they cross over each other to hide the folds and thread. All of the 2-1/2" flower petals will be sewn in this "pinch and fold" fashion. Pinch and fold the centers of four eggshell petals, and sew those into your lei, alternating the petals so they cross over each other to hide the folds and thread.

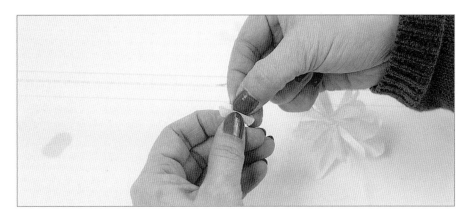

16) Fan fold, or "pinch," the center of a yellow petal into thirds lengthwise.

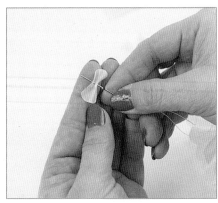

17) Poke your needle through the center of the petal, through all three thicknesses. Continue with another yellow petal. All of the yellow petals will be sewn in this "pinch" fashion, without the "fold."

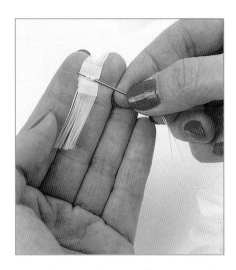

18) Take one of the shredded ribbon pieces, and open it up to reveal the spine and crease. Using a tiny running stitch, sew up the crease of the spine.

19) Gather the petals and the white stamen together. This will make one flower in your lei. Pull these petals down toward your knot at the end of the thread. Be sure to alternate the petals so they cross over each other to hide the folds and thread.

20) Continue with this series, using eight ivory, four eggshell, two yellow, and one white stamen, until your lei measures 40". (On your last flower, do not include the white stamen. It will be easier to tie the ends of your lei together if you don't have the shredded ribbon getting in your way.)

21) Tightly knot the needle end of the thread close against the ribbon. Cut needle off of the thread, approximately 3 to 4" away from the knot.

22) Tie both ends of the thread together to form your lei. Make several knots in the same place to prevent the thread from loosening. Trim the thread close to the knots. Tie a decorative ribbon bow on to your lei over your thread knots, to cover up this area and to complete your lei.

Lehua Pepa (Lehua Pepa detail)

Lehua Pepa (Bozu or Paper Ball)

—Materials Needed—

This lei design was created by Coreen Iwamoto of the San Francisco Bay Area.

- 10 yds. 5/8″ white satin ribbon
- 10 yds. 5/8″ fuchsia satin ribbon
- 10 yds. 5/8″ purple satin ribbon
- 10 ft. beading or upholstery thread
- Aoyama 1/8″ double-sided tape (optional)
- 1 sewing needle
- Scissors
- Marking pen (preferably gel-style to prevent spreading ink)
- Ruler

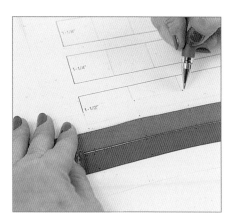

1) Lay the ribbons next to each other on top of or beside a ruler, wrong (dull) sides up. Allowing for a short amount of leader at the beginning of the ribbon, dot your ribbons at 1-1/2″ intervals down each edge of each ribbon, until all the ribbons have been marked. These are your stitching marks.

(Optional: If you want to make the cut edge of the ribbons resistant to fraying, attach a small piece of Aoyama 1/8″ double-sided tape to the wrong side of each cut edge, and fold over the edges to encase the tape, resulting in clean edges that won't ravel.)

Thread your sewing needle with the beading or upholstery thread, and bring cut ends together. Tie a double knot approximately 3 to 4″ from the cut ends. This amount of thread will allow you to complete a finished lei of 40″, with additional thread to easily tie the ends together.

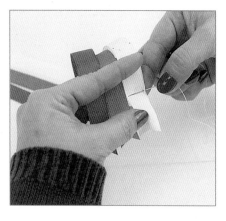

2) Line up the ribbons in your hand next to each other, cut edges closest to you and wrong sides up.

3) If you are right-handed, starting with the ribbon furthest to the right, bring your needle from behind the ribbon up through the right-most mark, then stitch down through the corresponding mark on the other edge of the ribbon, come up through the first mark of the second and down through the second, then up and down through the next ribbon. This is a running stitch.

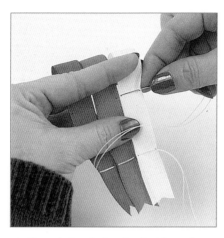

4) From behind the third ribbon, bring your needle above and in front of all three ribbons, and then your next stitch will be up through the next pen mark of the ribbon farthest to the right. You will then proceed with your running stitch through all three ribbons again, being sure to keep the order of the ribbons consistent.

5) Pull up on the thread so the ribbons go down the thread to the knotted end.

6) As you pull tighter, the ribbons will each form little puffs, or bozu flowers.

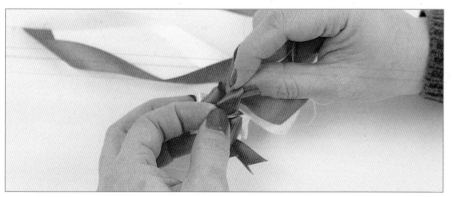

7) If the ribbons get stuck inside themselves, or into each other, pull them out or slightly apart to puff them out separately. You should now have one flower of each color. Your next stitches through all three colors will form flowers on the other side of your round lei and complete your first row of flowers.

8) As you continue on with this series of running stitches, pulling down, and puffing up of the flowers, the colors will form a long spiral up your lei.

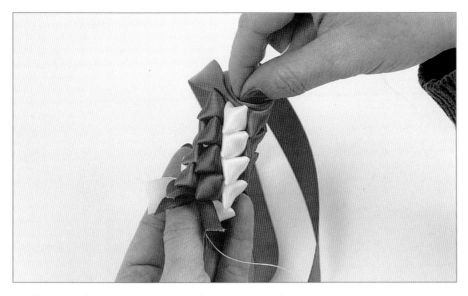

9) Continue this process until your lei measures 40".

10) Tightly knot the needle end of the thread close against the ribbon.

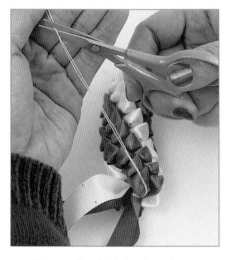

11) Cut needle off of the thread, approximately 3 to 4″ away from the knot.

12) Cut off the excess ribbons on the diagonal near the knot.

(Optional: If you want to make the cut edge of the ribbons resistant to fraying, attach a small piece of Aoyama 1/8″ double-sided tape to the wrong side of each cut edge, and fold over the edges to encase the tape, resulting in clean edges that won't ravel.)

13) Tie both ends of the thread together to form your lei. Make several knots in the same place to prevent the thread from loosening. Trim the thread close to the knots. Tie a decorative ribbon bow on to your lei over your thread knots, to cover up this area and to complete your lei.

Haku choker

Haku choker detail

Haku Choker

—Materials Needed—

- 2 yds. #3 (5/8″) red acetate ribbon
- 1 yd. #3 (5/8″) valeria acetate ribbon
- 2 yds. #3 (5/8″) belle acetate ribbon
- 1 yd. #3 (5/8″) golden yellow acetate ribbon
- 2 yds. #3 (5/8″) azalea acetate ribbon
- 1 yd. #3 (5/8″) pink acetate ribbon
- 2 yds. #3 (5/8″) purple acetate ribbon
- 1 yd. #3 (5/8″) Offray lavender acetate ribbon
- 2 yds. #3 (5/8″) white acetate ribbon
- 1 yd. #3 (5/8″) eggshell acetate ribbon
- 12-1/2 yds. #3 (5/8″) Offray moss or C&G basil acetate ribbon
- 1-1/3 yds. #3 (5/8″) yellow acetate ribbon
- 1/3 yd. #40 (2-1/2″) white acetate ribbon
- 1/2 yd. Aoyama 1/8″ double-sided tape
- 1 yd. 3/8″ black grosgrain ribbon
- 7 ft. beading or upholstery thread
- 2 20mm round wooden beads
- 1 sewing needle
- 1 sturdy needle (like a carpet needle)
- Scissors
- Ruler

1) This completed choker will display five color patterns of flowers (red, gold, pink, purple and white), interspersed with baby's breath and greenery. The colors listed are in the order shown in the photo. You may opt to use fewer colors, or more, depending on your preference. This is just an example of the variety of colors you can use to fashion your lei. This imitates real haku lei-making, where the creator can use any number of materials to make a stunning lei.

2) Lay the red acetate ribbon on top or beside a ruler. At 2″ intervals, fan-fold the ribbon back and forth, to mark your cutting lengths.

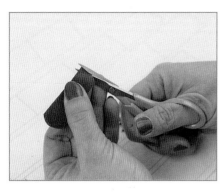  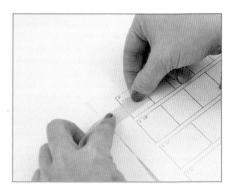

3) When you have a comfortable amount of ribbon folded, cut the folded edge in a half-circle shape. Repeat with the other side. Each cut piece is a petal of the flower. Continue cutting this 2" shape of the red, belle, azalea, purple, and white ribbons, to make at least 32 red, 32 belle, 32 azalea, 32 purple, and 32 white petals. Cut the same 2" shape of the valeria, golden yellow, pink, lavender and eggshell ribbons, to make at least 16 valeria, 16 golden yellow, 16 pink, 16 lavender, and 16 eggshell petals.

4) Measuring 1-3/4", cut the same shape of the basil ribbon, to make at least 450 basil petals.

5) Measuring 1", cut the same shape of the yellow ribbon, to make at least 40 yellow petals.

6) Now you will make the baby's breath flowers. Measuring 2", fan-fold the white ribbon to create six "panels."

7) Cut the ribbon, which should measure 12" total.

8) Open up the folded white ribbon, fold down its center line, wrong sides together, and crease down this 12" length.

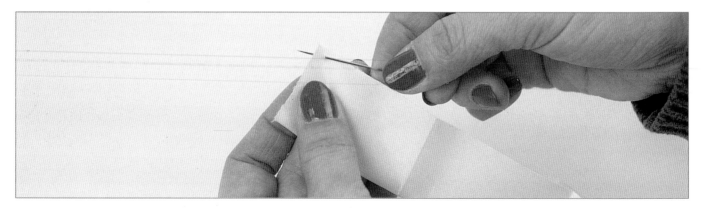

9) Hold the creased edge in your hand, while the other holds the sturdy needle. You are going to shred the edge of the ribbon. Poke the needle near the upper right corner of the ribbon, through both thicknesses. Pull needle away from your other hand, allowing the long strands of the ribbon to pull away with it. Repeat a little further down the long edge of the ribbon, pulling away to reveal more of the loose strands.

10) When you have pulled away enough of the loose strands to grasp them in your hand, pull them away from the rest of the ribbon. Continue with the shredding, pulling away about 1/8" of strands at a time (pulling more may rip the strands as they pull away from the ribbon). Continue until you leave about 1/4" of intact ribbon, on each side of the long crease.

11) At each 2" interval you originally fan-folded, cut the 1/4" "spine." You should have six 2" pieces. (The markings on the ribbon should not be made on your lei; they are merely indications of the measurements you will be cutting.)

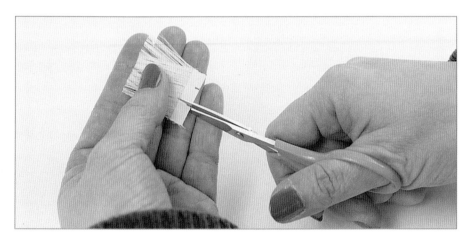

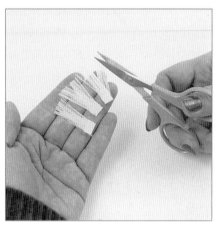

12) For each of these 2" pieces, cut in half to yield twelve 1" pieces.

13) Each of the 1" pieces should be cut into thirds. You should now have six pieces of 1/3" shred from that initial 2" panel of ribbon. The full length of white ribbon will result in 36 1/3" pieces.

Thread your sewing needle with the beading or upholstery thread, and bring cut ends together. Tie a double knot approximately 5 to 6" from the cut ends. This amount of thread will allow you to complete a finished choker of 24", with additional thread for the ties at both ends.

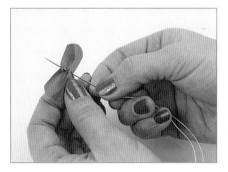

14) You will start and end this lei with the basil ribbon petals, indicating our "greenery" for this lei. Fan-fold, or "pinch," the center of a basil petal into thirds lengthwise.

15) Poke your needle through the center of the petal, through all three thicknesses.

16) Continue with eleven more basil petals. All of the basil petals will be sewn in this "pinch" fashion.

17) Pull these basil petals down toward your knot at the end of the thread. Be sure to alternate the petals so they cross over each other to hide the folds and thread.

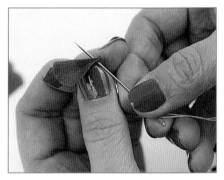

18) Now you will start your first "flower" in your lei. Each flower will have eight petals, followed by two yellow petals, then four complementary-colored petals, and completed with a shredded white piece. As you did for the basil petal, pinch the center of a red petal into thirds.

19) Fold this in half crosswise into a tight "V" shape.

20) Poke your needle through all six thicknesses. Repeat with seven more red petals, alternating the petals so they cross over each other to hide the folds and thread. All of the 2″ flower petals will be sewn in this "pinch and fold" fashion.

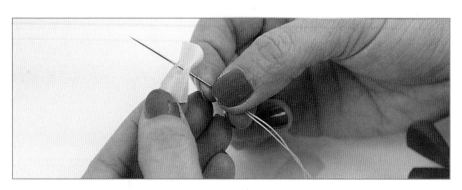

21) As you did for the basil petal, pinch the center of a yellow petal into thirds. Sew through the center of the petal, through all three thicknesses. Repeat with a second yellow petal. All of the 1″ yellow petals will be sewn in this "pinch" fashion.

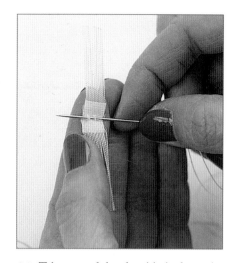

22) As you did for the red petal, pinch and fold the centers of each of the valeria petals and sew through all six thicknesses, alternating how each petal is laid over the previous one to hide the folds and thread.

23) Gather the red, yellow and valeria petals together. This completes the petals of one flower in your lei. You will now add the baby's breath.

24) Take one of the shredded white ribbon pieces, and open it up to reveal the spine and crease. Using a tiny running stitch, sew up the crease of the spine.

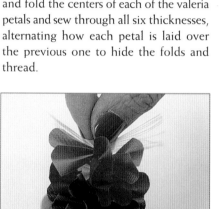

25) Pull the flower down toward your first bunch of greenery. Sew up another bunch of greenery. Continue with the different-colored flowers for your lei, separating each by a bunch of greenery.

26) Your next flower will be the belle/golden yellow combination. Use eight belle, two yellow, four golden yellow, and one white shred.

27) Your next flower will be the azalea/pink combination. Use eight azalea, two yellow, four pink, and one white shred.

28) Your next flower will be the purple/lavender combination. Use eight purple, two yellow, four lavender, and one white shred.

29) Your next flower will be the white/eggshell combination. Use eight white, two yellow, four eggshell, and one white shred.

30) This makes one complete cycle of flower colors, which measures approximately 6″. Repeat this cycle, or mix up the colors if you want the pattern to appear random. Continue this process until your lei measures 24 to 25″.

31) Tightly knot the needle end of the thread close against the ribbon.

32) Cut needle off of the thread, approximately 5 to 6″ away from the knot.

33) Cut your grosgrain ribbon in half crosswise, to yield two 18″ pieces.

34) Fold each of the pieces in half crosswise, wrong sides together, so you have two 9″ folded pieces. These will encase your loose threads and become your ties.

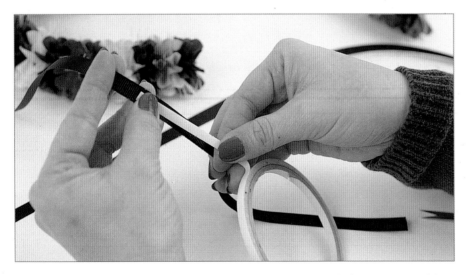

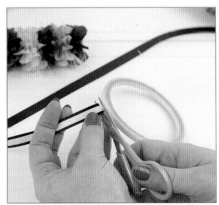

35) Using your Aoyama double-sided tape, line the inside of the grosgrain ribbon down the center, from fold to cut edge.

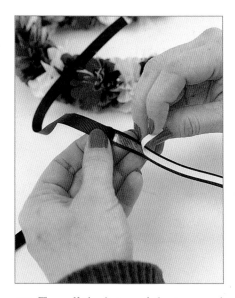

36) Tear off the lining of the tape, and lay the loose thread from one side of your lei along the tape, with your thread knot near the cut edge of the grosgrain.

37) Make sure the thread runs down the center of the ribbon along the double-sided tape.

38) Using the other cut edge of the grosgrain that doesn't have the tape affixed, lay that cut edge on top of the other cut edge, and smooth the two sides of the ribbon together, encasing the loose thread from your lei inside.

39) Repeat with other side of the lei and the remaining grosgrain ribbon.

40) String a wooden bead on to one of the ties, pulling it toward the cut edges of the grosgrain. Tie a knot in the grosgrain tie to secure the wooden bead on to the tie. This will hide the raw edge of the grosgrain and the thread.

41) Repeat with the other wooden bead on the other tie.

Pahūpahū (Pahūpahū detail)

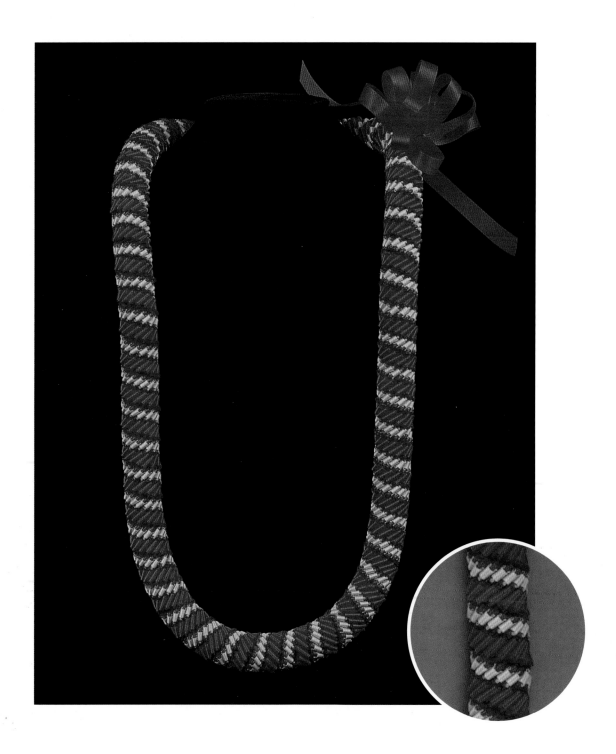

Pahūpahū (Firecracker)

—Materials Needed—

This lei design was created by Carole Mito of Honolulu.

- 40 yds. 3/16″ light gold (or yellow) picot ribbon
- 40 yds. 3/8″ red picot ribbon
- 10 fts. beading or upholstery thread
- 1 sewing needle
- Scissors

Thread your sewing needle with the beading or upholstery thread, and bring cut ends together. Tie a double knot approximately 3 to 4″ from the cut ends. This amount of thread will allow you to complete a finished lei of 40″, with additional thread to easily tie the ends together.

1) Lay the red picot ribbon in your hand, cut edge closest to you and wrong side up. Lay the yellow picot ribbon on top of the red, right side up. Line up the ribbons along their center lines so you can see the red ribbon on both sides of the yellow ribbon. You will regulate your stitch length by counting the loops along one edge of the yellow ribbon. Each stitch will be six loops after the last stitch, which should equate to 1″ intervals. Be sure to count only on one edge of the ribbon, since these loops typically alternate and do not line up equally on both edges of the ribbon.

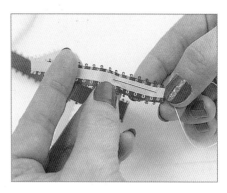

2) Stitching along the center lines of both ribbons, poke needle up through both thicknesses. Your next stitch will be six loops away from that stitch, through the center lines of both thicknesses.

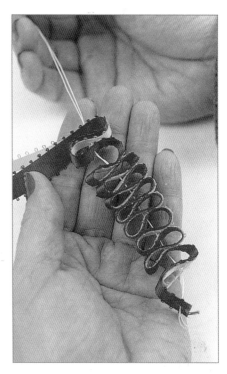

3) Continue with this running stitch pattern for several more stitches.

4) Firmly gather the sewn ribbon down the thread until you reach the knotted end.

5) Holding both ends of the gathered ribbon, twist the gathers, with one hand turning toward you and the other hand turning outward, to start a "candy cane" pattern to the ribbon.

6) Continue this process, with several more running stitches, gathering, and twisting.

7) Be sure to push down the ribbon toward the knotted end as you twist, to ensure a consistently tight pattern.

8) Continue this process until your lei measures 40".

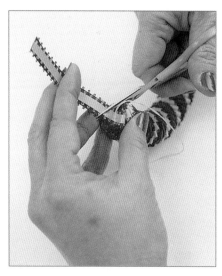

9) Tightly knot the needle end of the thread close against the ribbon. Cut needle off of the thread, approximately 3 to 4" away from the knot. Cut off the excess ribbons on the diagonal near the knot.

10) Tie both ends of the thread together to form your lei.

11) Make several knots in the same place to prevent the thread from loosening. Trim the thread close to the knots.

12) Tie a decorative ribbon bow on to your lei over your thread knots, to cover up this area and to complete your lei.

'Ohai Ali'i 'Ula'ula

'Ohai Ali'i 'Ula'ula detail

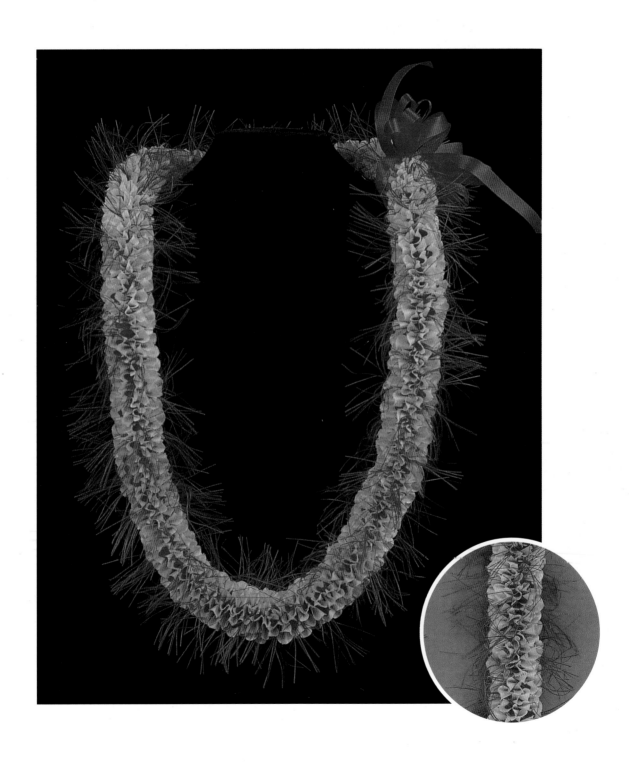

'Ohai Ali'i 'Ula'ula (Red Poinciana)

—Materials Needed—

This lei design was created by Coryn Tanaka of Honolulu.

- 20 yds. #3 (5/8") Offray or C&G belle acetate ribbon
- 20 yds. #3 (5/8") C&G golden yellow acetate ribbon
- 14 yds. #3 (5/8") red acetate ribbon
- 1-1/2 yds. #100 (4") red acetate ribbon
- 10 ft. beading or upholstery thread
- 1 sewing needle
- 1 sturdy needle (like a carpet needle)
- Scissors
- Ruler

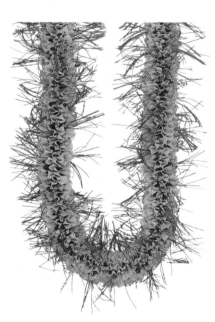

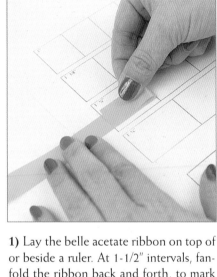

1) Lay the belle acetate ribbon on top of or beside a ruler. At 1-1/2" intervals, fan-fold the ribbon back and forth, to mark your cutting lengths.

2) When you have a comfortable amount of ribbon folded, cut the folded edge in a half-circle shape. Repeat with the other side. Continue cutting this 1-1/2" shape of the belle and golden yellow ribbons, to make at least 480 belle pieces, or petals, and 480 golden yellow petals.

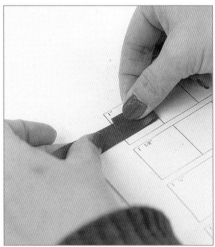

3) Measuring 1", cut the same shape of the #3 red ribbon, to make at least 480 red petals.

4) These are the three main petals for your flowers. You will now prepare the stamens.

5) Measuring 2″, fan fold the #100 red ribbon to create six "panels."

6) Cut the ribbon, which should measure 12″ total.

7) Open up the folded red ribbon, fold down its center line, wrong sides together, and crease down this 12″ length.

8) Hold the creased edge in your hand, while the other holds the sturdy needle. You are going to shred the ends of the ribbon. Poke the needle near the upper right corner of the ribbon, through both thicknesses.

9) Pull needle away from your other hand, allowing the long strands of the ribbon to pull away with it. Repeat a little further down the long edge of the ribbon, pulling away to reveal more of the loose strands.

10) When you have pulled away enough of the loose strands to grasp them in your hand, pull them away from the rest of the ribbon.

11) Continue with the shredding, pulling away about 1/8″ of strands at a time (pulling more may rip the strands as they pull away from the ribbon). Continue until you leave about 1/4″ of intact ribbon, on each side of the long crease.

12) At each 2″ interval you originally fan-folded, cut the 1/4″ "spine". You should have six 2″ pieces. (The markings on the ribbon should not be made on your lei; they are merely indications of the measurements you will be cutting.)

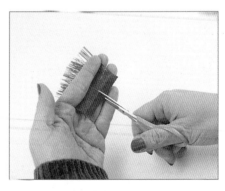

13) For each of these 2″ pieces, cut in half to yield twelve 1″ pieces.

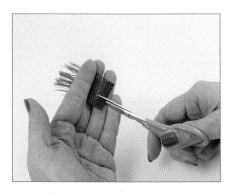

14) Each of the 1″ pieces should be cut into thirds. You should now have 6 pieces of 1/3″ shred from that initial 2″ panel of ribbon. These represent the stamens of the flower. Repeat with additional 12″ sections of #100 red ribbon as needed.

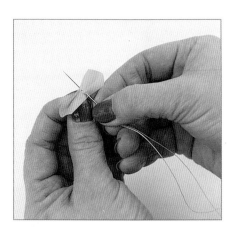

16) Poke your needle through the center of the petal, through all three thicknesses. Continue with one more belle petal. All of the petals will be sewn in this "pinch" fashion.

Thread your sewing needle with the beading or upholstery thread, and bring cut ends together. Tie a double knot approximately 3 to 4″ from the cut ends. This amount of thread will allow you to complete a finished lei of 40″, with additional thread to easily tie the ends together.

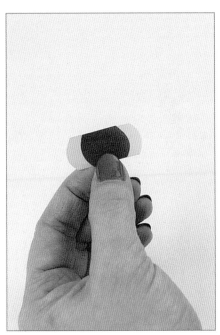

17) Center a red petal on top of a golden yellow petal.

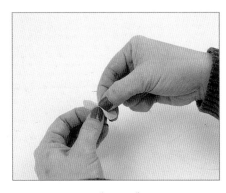

15) Fan-fold, or "pinch," the center of a belle petal into thirds lengthwise.

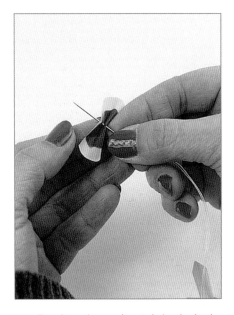

18) Pinch and sew through both thicknesses of the centers of these petals. Repeat with another red/golden yellow petal combination.

19) Repeat with two more belle pieces, then two more golden yellow/red combination pieces. This results in this pattern, and completes the petals for one flower. You will now attach a stamen.

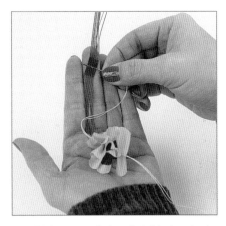

20) Take one of the shredded red ribbon pieces, and open it up to reveal the spine and crease. Using a tiny running stitch, sew up the crease of the spine.

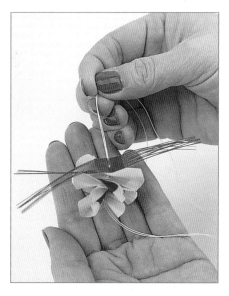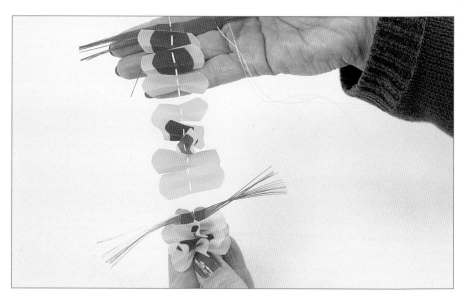

21) Gather the petals and red stamen together. This will make one flower in your lei. Pull these petals down toward your knot at the end of the thread. Be sure to alternate the petals so they cross over each other to hide the folds and thread.

22) Continue with this series, using two belle, then two red/golden yellow combinations, then two more belle, then two more red/golden yellow combinations, and one red stamen, until your lei measures 40".

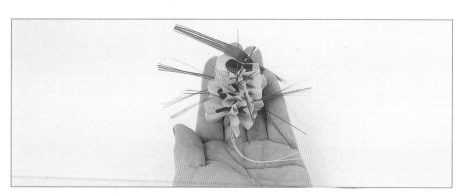

23) On your last flower, do not include the red stamen. It will be easier to tie the ends of your lei together if you don't have the shredded ribbon getting in your way.

24) Tightly knot the needle end of the thread close against the ribbon. Cut needle off of the thread, approximately 3 to 4" away from the knot.

25) Tie both ends of the thread together to form your lei. Make several knots in the same place to prevent the thread from loosening. Trim the thread close to the knots. Tie a decorative ribbon bow on to your lei over your thread knots, to cover up this area and to complete your lei.

Nani-o-'Ōla'a

Nani-o-'Ōla'a detail

Nani-o-'Ōla'a ('Ōla'a Beauty)

—Materials Needed—

This lei design was created by Coreen Iwamoto of the San Francisco Bay Area.

- 31 yds. #3 (5/8″) Offray grappa or C&G aubergine acetate ribbon
- 6.5 yds. #3 (5/8″) black acetate ribbon
- 9.5 yds. #3 (5/8″) lavender acetate ribbon
- 9.5 yds. #3 (5/8″) purple acetate ribbon
- 5 yds. #3 (5/8″) yellow acetate ribbon
- 10 ft. beading or upholstery thread
- 1 sewing needle
- Scissors
- Ruler

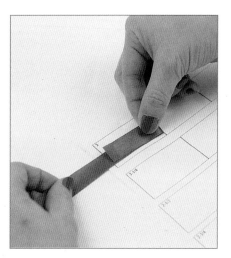

1) Lay the aubergine acetate ribbon on top or beside a ruler.

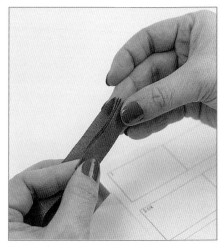

2) At 2″ intervals, fan-fold the ribbon back and forth, to mark your cutting lengths.

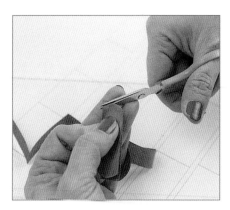

3) When you have a comfortable amount of ribbon folded, cut the folded edge in a half-circle shape. Repeat with the other side. Continue cutting this 2″ shape of the aubergine ribbons, to make at least 560 aubergine pieces, or petals. Cut this 2″ shape of the lavender and purple ribbons, to make at least 168 lavender and 168 purple petals. Cut this 2″ shape of the black ribbon, to make at least 112 black petals.

4) Measuring 1-1/2″, cut the same shape of the yellow ribbon, to make at least 112 yellow petals.

Thread your sewing needle with the beading or upholstery thread, and bring cut ends together. Tie a double knot approximately 3 to 4" from the cut ends. This amount of thread will allow you to complete a finished lei of 40", with additional thread to easily tie the ends together.

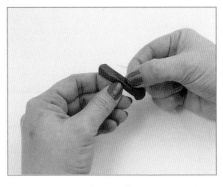

5) Fan-fold, or "pinch," the center of an aubergine petal into thirds.

6) Fold this in half crosswise into a tight "V" shape.

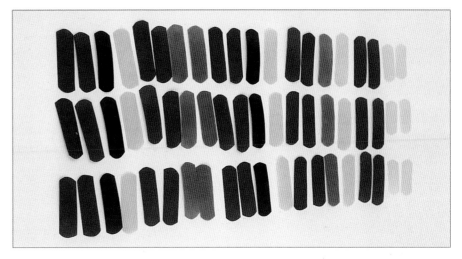

7) Poke your needle through all six thicknesses. Repeat with another aubergine petal, alternating the petals so they cross over each other to hide the folds and thread. All of the 2" flower petals will be sewn in this "pinch and fold" fashion.

8) Pinch and fold in this order: 2 aubergine (which you just completed), 1 black, 1 lavender, 2 aubergine, 2 purple, 2 aubergine, 1 black, 1 lavender, 2 aubergine, 1 purple, 1 lavender, 2 aubergine. The last two petals will be 2 yellow pieces, which are sewn slightly differently (as follows). The rows of pieces shown here will make 3 complete patterns on your lei.

9) Here is a lavender petal formed with the pinch and fold fashion.

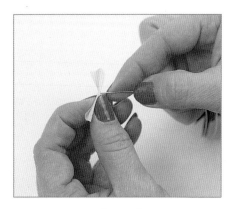

10) Fan-fold, or "pinch," the center of a yellow petal into thirds lengthwise. Poke your needle through the center of the petal, through all three thicknesses. Repeat with another yellow petal. All of the yellow petals will be sewn in this "pinch" fashion.

11) Gather the petals together. This will make one pattern in your lei. Pull these petals down toward your knot at the end of the thread.

12) Be sure to alternate the petals so they cross over each other to hide the folds and thread.

13) Note that the colors of the petals appear randomly dispersed through the lei. Continue with this series until your lei measures 40".

14) Tightly knot the needle end of the thread close against the ribbon. Cut needle off of the thread, approximately 3 to 4" away from the knot.

15) Tie both ends of the thread together to form your lei. Trim the thread close to the knots. Make several knots in the same place to prevent the thread from loosening.

16) Tie a decorative ribbon bow on to your lei over your thread knots, to cover up this area and to complete your lei.

Hinahina choker

Hinahina choker detail

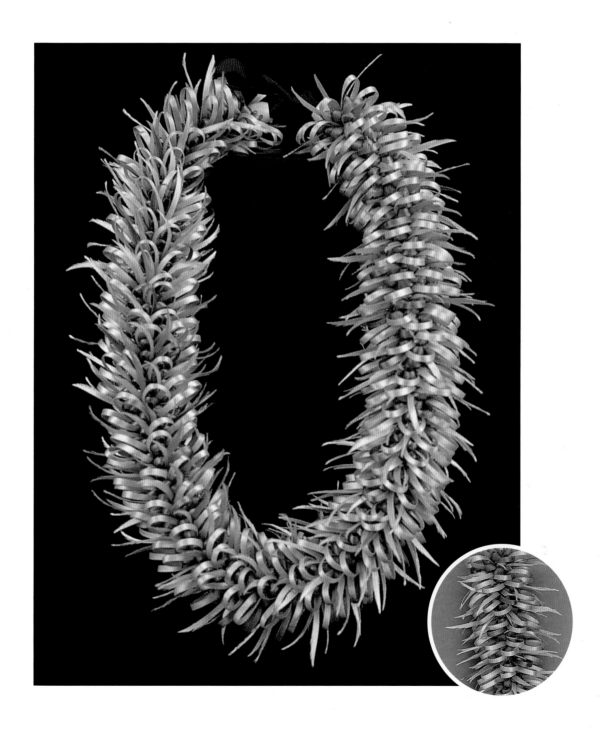

Hinahina Choker (Spanish moss)

—Materials Needed—

This lei design was created by Carole Mito of Honolulu.

- 28 to 30 yd. 3/16" old willow picot ribbon
- 5 yds. 1/8" moss satin ribbon (slightly darker than the old willow color)
- 50 yds. 1/8" silver satin ribbon
- Marking pen (preferably gel-style to prevent spreading ink)
- 7 ft. beading or upholstery thread
- 1 sewing needle
- Scissors
- Ruler
- 1 wooden clothespin with metal spring
- 1/2 yd. Aoyama 1/8" double-sided tape
- 1 yd. 3/8" black grosgrain ribbon
- 2 20mm round wooden beads

1) Lay the moss satin ribbon on top of or beside a ruler, right side up. Allowing for a short amount of leader at the beginning of the ribbon, dot your ribbon at 2-1/2" intervals down the center of the ribbon.

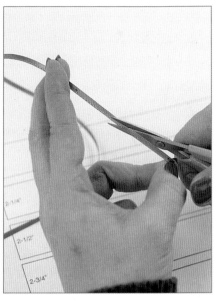

2) Halfway between the first and second dots, cut the ribbon on a sharp diagonal.

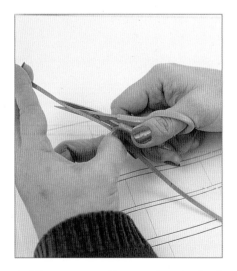

3) The next cut will occur after the third dot beyond your initial cut. Continue to mark and cut these segments.

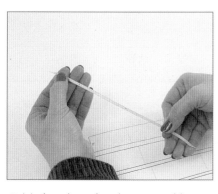

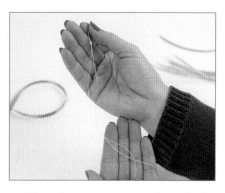

4) Mark and cut the silver satin ribbon in the same manner as the moss satin ribbon. You will have ten silver segments for every one moss segment.

5) Lay the old willow picot ribbon on top of or beside a ruler, right side up. Allowing for a short amount of leader at the beginning of the ribbon, dot your ribbon at 1-1/4″ intervals down the center of the ribbon, until all the ribbon has been marked. These are your stitching marks on your lei base.

6) Thread your sewing needle with the beading or upholstery thread, and bring cut ends together. Tie a double knot approximately 5 to 6″ from the cut ends. This amount of thread will allow you to complete a finished choker of 24 to 25″.

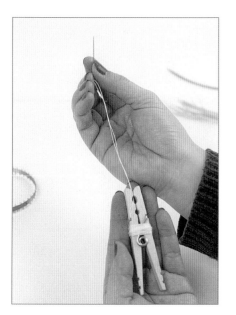

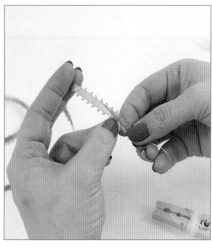

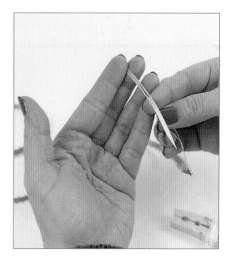

7) Starting from the knotted end of the thread, wind the thread around the center of the clothespin until your thread measures about 4 to 5″ from the needle. Secure the thread in the pincher of the clothespin. You will be working with only 4 to 5″ of thread at a time, letting out additional thread as necessary and pushing the finished petals of the lei downward toward the clothespin as you go.

8) Lay the picot ribbon in your hand, cut edge closest to you and right side up. Stitching in the center of the ribbon, poke the needle up through the first marking. Pull needle toward you while you pull the ribbon away from you (the clothespin should be kept free and dangling—this will keep a weight on your thread, and prevent tangling of the thread with your ribbon and lei design).

9) Take a silver segment and poke the needle up through its first marking.

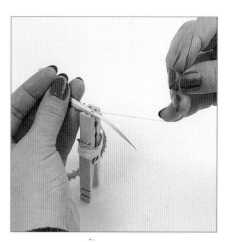

10) Align the two ribbons together so they will both follow the same general path as you make your "petal" loops.

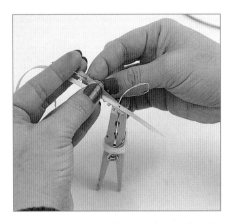

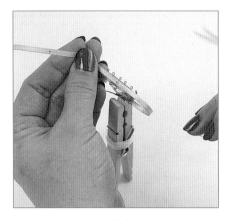

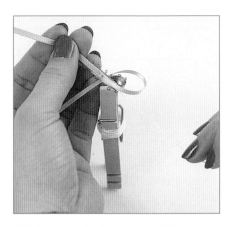

11) Bring your needle up and over the ribbon, and then your next stitch will be up through the next marking on the picot ribbon. Poke your needle up through the next marking on the silver segment.

12) Be sure to pull the needle toward you, ribbon away from you, with the clothespin dangling.

13) As you pull, the ribbon will form the first of five petals in a loop.

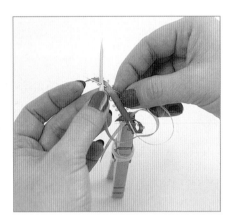

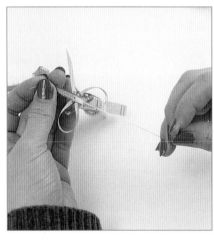

14) Continue with the next stitch, consistently bringing needle up through the two ribbons through the markings, and then pulling needle and ribbon in opposite directions, to form your second loop.

15) This ends the markings on the silver segment.

16) Stitch up through the next marking on the picot ribbon.

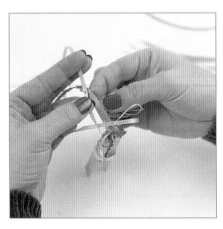

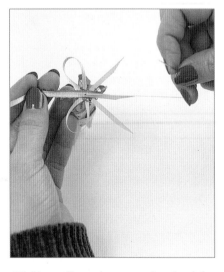

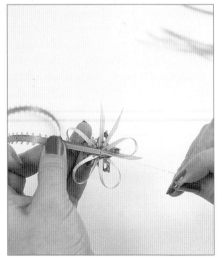

17) You will now add another silver segment onto your lei. Stitch up through the first marking on a new silver segment, again pulling needle and ribbon to form the third loop.

18) You will see the pointed ends of the silver segments sticking out of your lei as accents.

19) The next two stitches continue in this pattern, resulting in a five-point star shape.

20) The next petal (#6) will start the next row. This petal will be situated between 2 petals in the previous row. This next row of five petals will alternate with the first row's petals, and your lei will continue on in this star-shaped, alternating pattern.

21) After you have placed ten silver segments into your lei, the next segment will be a moss segment. Join this into your lei in the same sewing pattern as before. Then continue on with the next set of ten silver and one moss.

22) As you continue creating rows of petals, you will find that your thread is now too short to continue stitching. Let out a few more inches of thread from the clothespin and clamp it. Gently pull the petals, a little bit at a time, down the thread toward the clothespin.

23) You now have more available thread with which to continue sewing. Continue this process until your lei measures 24 to 25".

24) Tightly knot the needle end of the thread close against the ribbon.

25) Cut off excess old willow picot ribbon on the diagonal near the knot. Cut needle off of the thread, approximately 5 to 6" away from the knot.

26) Cut your grosgrain ribbon in half crosswise, to yield two 18" pieces.

27) Fold each of the pieces in half crosswise, wrong sides together, so you have two 9" folded pieces. These will encase your loose threads and become your ties.

28) Using your Aoyama double-sided tape, line the inside of the grosgrain ribbon down the center, from fold to cut edge.

29) Tear off the lining of the tape, and lay the loose thread from one side of your lei along the tape, with your thread knot near the cut edge of the grosgrain.

30) Make sure the thread runs down the center of the ribbon along the double-sided tape.

31) Using the other cut edge of the grosgrain that doesn't have the tape affixed, lay that cut edge on top of the other cut edge, and smooth the two sides of the ribbon together, encasing the loose thread from your lei inside. Repeat with other side of the lei and the remaining grosgrain ribbon.

32) String a wooden bead onto one of the ties, pulling it toward the cut edges of the grosgrain.

33) Tie a knot in the grosgrain tie to secure the wooden bead to the tie. This will hide the raw edge of the grosgrain and the thread. Repeat with the other wooden bead on the other tie.

Ponimō'ī

Ponimō'ī detail

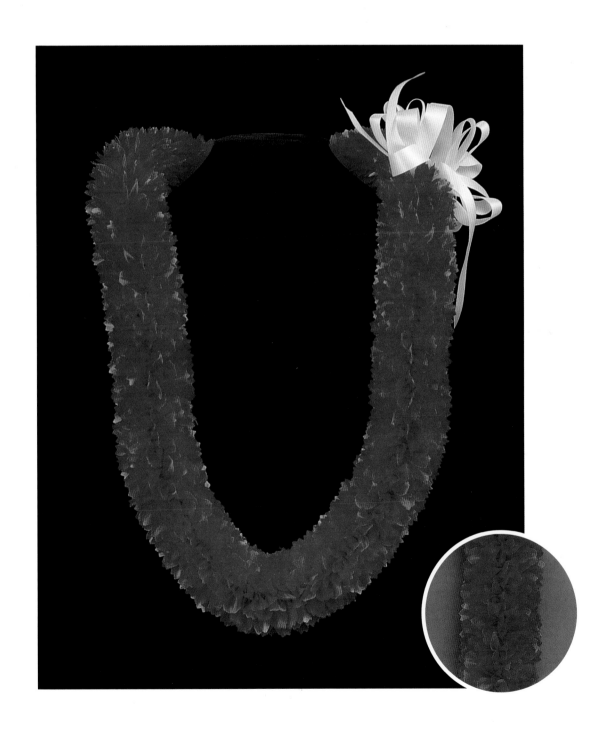

Ponimō‘ī (Carnation)

This lei design was created by Coreen Iwamoto of the San Francisco Bay Area.

- 45 yds. #3 (5/8″) red acetate ribbon
- 23 yds. #3 (5/8″) valeria acetate ribbon
- 10 ft. beading or uphol- stery thread
- 1 sewing needle
- Scissors
- Pinking shears
- Ruler

1) Lay the red acetate ribbon on top of or beside a ruler.

2) At 2-1/2″ intervals, fan-fold the ribbon back and forth, to mark your cutting lengths.

3) When you have a comfortable amount of ribbon folded, cut the folded edge using the pinking shears.

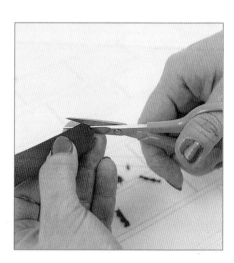

4) Using the regular scissors, round off the outer edges. Repeat with the other side.

Thread your sewing needle with the beading or upholstery thread, and bring cut ends together. Tie a double knot approximately 3 to 4" from the cut ends. This amount of thread will allow you to complete a finished lei of 40", with additional thread to easily tie the ends together.

5) Continue cutting this 2-1/2" shape of the red and valeria ribbons, to make at least 1,600 red and 800 valeria pieces, or petals.

6) Fan-fold, or "pinch," the center of a red petal into thirds lengthwise.

7) Fold this in half crosswise into a tight "V" shape.

8) Poke your needle through all six thicknesses. Repeat with seven more red petals, alternating the petals so they cross over each other to hide the folds and thread. All of the petals will be sewn in this "pinch and fold" fashion.

9) Pinch and fold the centers of four valeria petals, and sew those into your lei, alternating the petals so they cross over each other to hide the folds and thread.

10) Gather the petals together. This will make one flower in your lei. Pull these petals down toward your knot at the end of the thread.

11) Be sure to alternate the petals so they cross over each other to hide the folds and thread. Continue with this series, using eight red and four valeria petals, until your lei measures 40".

12) Tightly knot the needle end of the thread close against the ribbon. Cut needle off of the thread, approximately 3 to 4" away from the knot.

13) Tie both ends of the thread together to form your lei. Make several knots in the same place to prevent the thread from loosening. Trim the thread close to the knots. Tie a decorative ribbon bow on to your lei over your thread knots to cover up this area and to complete your lei.

Kīkā (Kīkā detail)

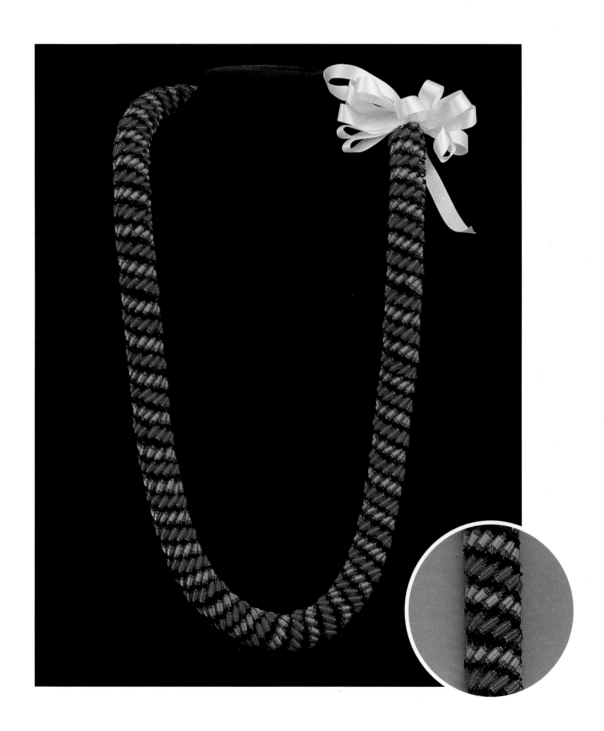

Kīkā (Cigar)

—Materials Needed—

This lei design was created by Carole Mito of Honolulu.

- 40 yds. 3/16″ orange picot ribbon
- 40 yds. 3/8″ seal brown picot ribbon
- 40 yds. 3/16″ red picot ribbon
- 10 ft. beading or upholstery thread
- 1 sewing needle
- Scissors
- Marking pen (preferably gel-style to prevent spreading ink)
- Ruler

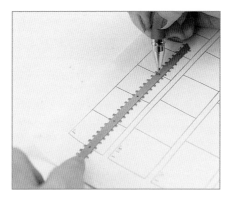

1) Lay the orange picot ribbon on top of or beside a ruler, right side up. Allowing for a short leader of approximately 1/4″ to 1/2″ at the beginning of the ribbon, dot your ribbon at 1″ intervals down the center of the ribbon, until all the orange ribbon has been marked. These are your stitching marks.

2) Lay the red picot ribbon in your hand, cut edge closest to you and wrong side up. Lay the brown picot ribbon on top of the red, right side up. Lay the orange picot ribbon on top of the brown, right side up. Line up the ribbons along their center lines so you can see the brown ribbon on both sides of the orange and red ribbons.

Thread your sewing needle with the beading or upholstery thread, and bring cut ends together. Tie a double knot approximately 3 to 4″ from the cut ends. This amount of thread will allow you to complete a finished lei of 40″, with additional thread to easily tie the ends together.

3) Stitching through the center lines of all three ribbons, poke needle through all three thicknesses, coming up through the pen mark on the orange ribbon.

4) Your next stitch will be down through the next pen mark through the center lines of all three thicknesses. This view is from behind, ensuring the stitch goes through the center lines.

5) Continue with this running stitch pattern for several more stitches.

6) Firmly gather the sewn ribbon down the thread until you reach the knotted end.

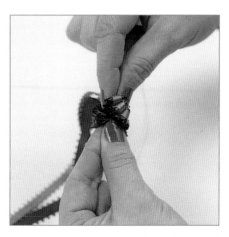

7) Holding both ends of the gathered ribbon, twist the gathers, with one hand

turning toward you and the other hand turning outward, to start a "candy cane" pattern to the ribbon.

8) Be sure to push down the ribbon toward the knotted end as you twist, to ensure a consistently tight pattern.

9) Continue this process, with several more running stitches, gathering, and twisting, until your lei measures 40".

67

10) Tightly knot the needle end of the thread close against the ribbon. Cut needle off of the thread, approximately 3 to 4″ away from the knot.

11) Cut off the excess ribbon on the diagonal near the knot.

12) Tie both ends of the thread together to form your lei. Make several knots in the same place to prevent the thread from loosening. Trim the thread close to the knots. Tie a decorative ribbon bow on to your lei over your thread knots, to cover up this area and to complete your lei.

Alahe'e-Haole

Alahe'e-Haole detail

Alahe'e Haole/Kukui
(Mock Orange/Candlenut)

—Materials Needed—

- 25 yds. #5 (7/8") Offray moss or C&G basil acetate ribbon
- 24 to 25 polished black kukui nuts, with holes drilled for stringing
- 10 ft. beading or upholstery thread
- 1 sewing needle
- Scissors
- Ruler

1) Lay the ribbon on top of or beside a ruler.

2) At 2" intervals, fan-fold the ribbon back and forth, to mark your cutting lengths.

Thread your sewing needle with the beading or upholstery thread, and bring cut ends together. Tie a double knot approximately 3 to 4" from the cut ends. This amount of thread will allow you to complete a finished lei of 40", with additional thread to easily tie the ends together.

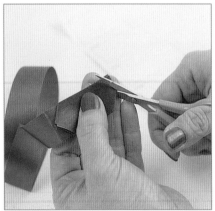

3) When you have a comfortable amount of ribbon folded, cut the folded edge in a "V" shape to taper to a point. Repeat with the other side. Continue cutting this 2" shape of the moss ribbon, to make at least 400 pieces, or leaves. Arrange your kukui nuts by size, going from smallest (#1 in order) to largest (#13) and then back down to the smallest (#24 or 25).

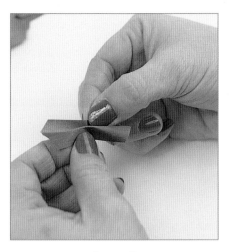

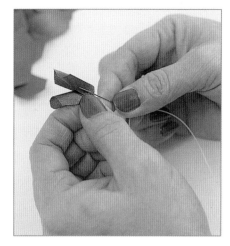

4) Fan-fold, or "pinch," the center of a leaf into thirds lengthwise.

5) Fold this in half crosswise into a tight "V" shape.

6) Poke your needle through all six thicknesses.

7) Repeat with fifteen more leaves, alternating them as they are sewn so they cross over each other to hide the folds and thread. All of the leaves will be sewn in this "pinch and fold" fashion.

8) Gather the sixteen leaves together and push them toward the knotted end of the thread.

9) String the first (smallest) kukui nut on to the thread and down toward the first batch of leaves.

10) Continue sewing the sixteen-leaf batches of greenery, and then a kukui nut, until your lei measures 40". Be sure to end your lei with a batch of greenery, which will make it easier to knot the end of the lei without a nut falling off.

11) Tightly knot the needle end of the thread close against the ribbon. Cut needle off of the thread, approximately 3 to 4″ away from the knot.

12) Tie both ends of the thread together to form your lei. Make several knots in the same place to prevent the thread from loosening. Trim the thread close to the knots. Tie a decorative ribbon bow on to your lei over your thread knots, to cover up this area and to complete your lei.

Bibliography

Pukui, Mary Kawena and Elbert, Samuel H.; *Hawaiian Dictionary: Hawaiian-English, English-Hawaiian*; University of Hawai'i Press, Honolulu, 1986.

Pukui, Mary Kawena, Elbert, Samuel H. and Mookini, Esther T.; *Place Names of Hawai'i (revised & expanded edition)*; University of Hawai'i Press, Honolulu, 1974.

Ide, Laurie Shimizu, *Hawaiian Lei Making—Step-by-Step Guide;* Mutual Publishing, Honolulu, 1998.